I0485601

Delicate Designs

And Beautiful Mandala

Adult Coloring book

By

S.B. Nozaz

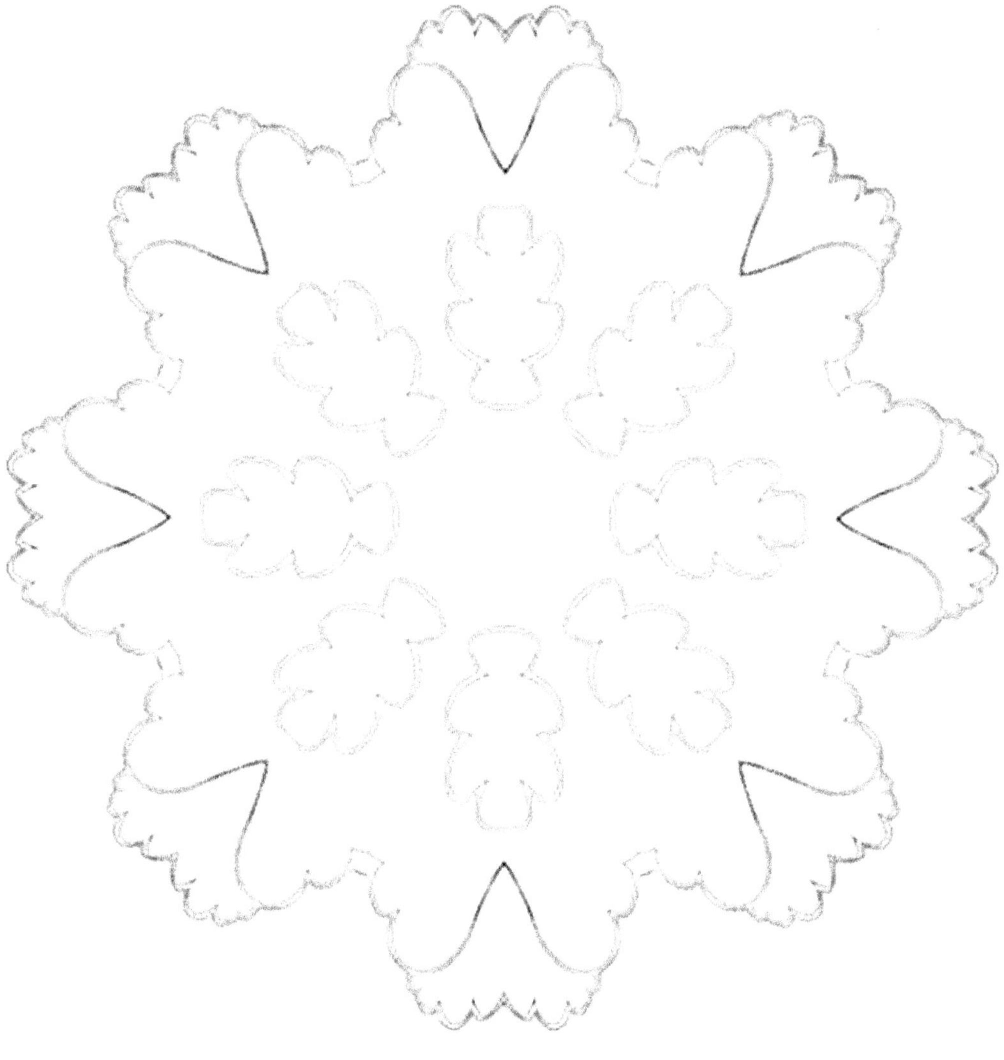

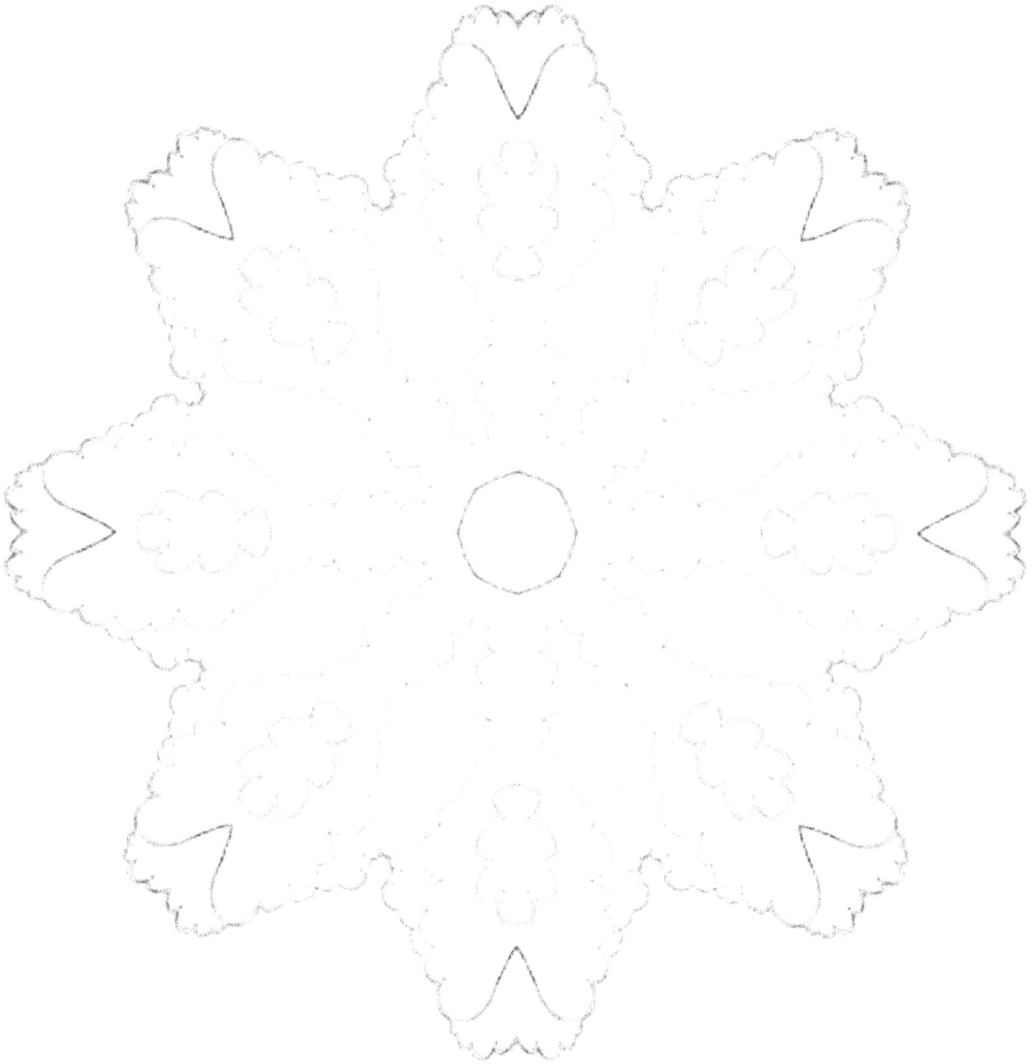

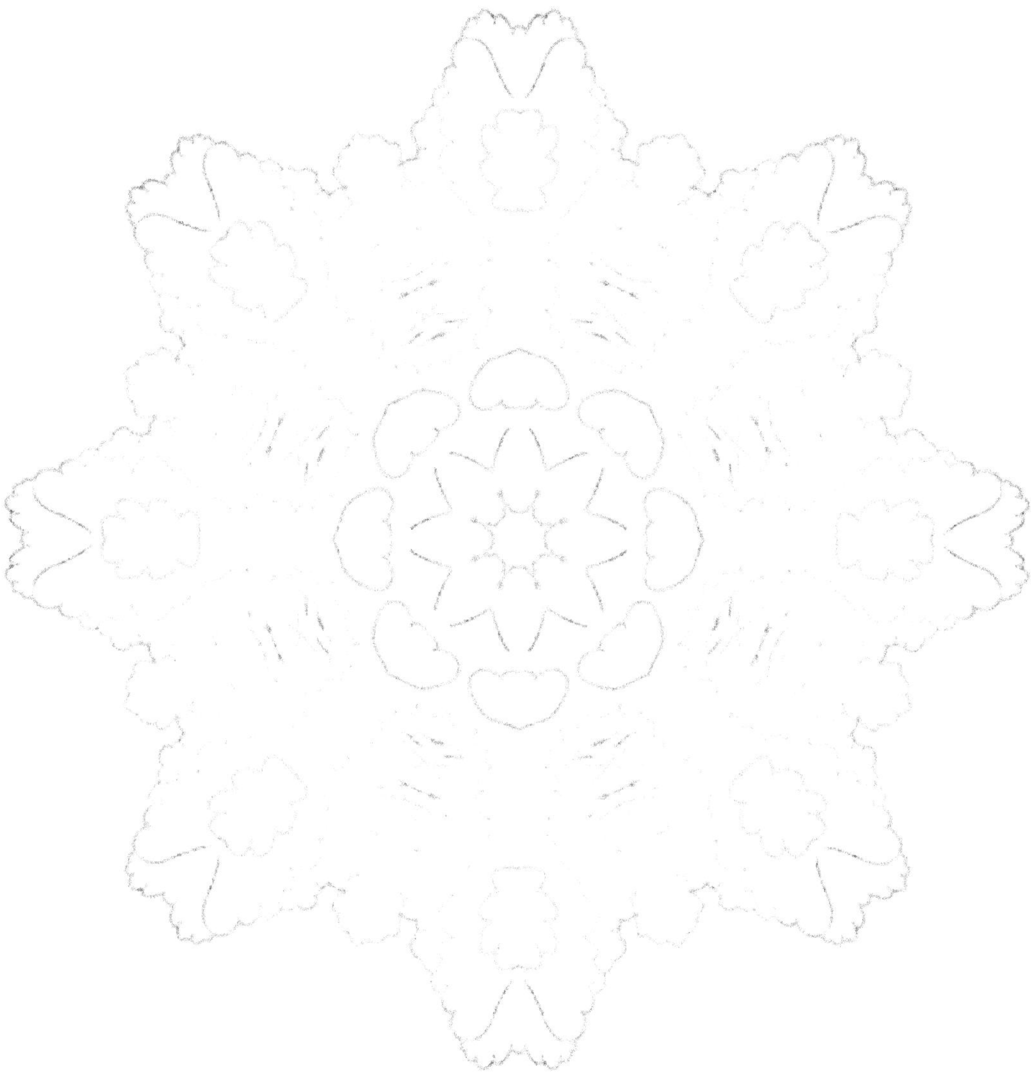

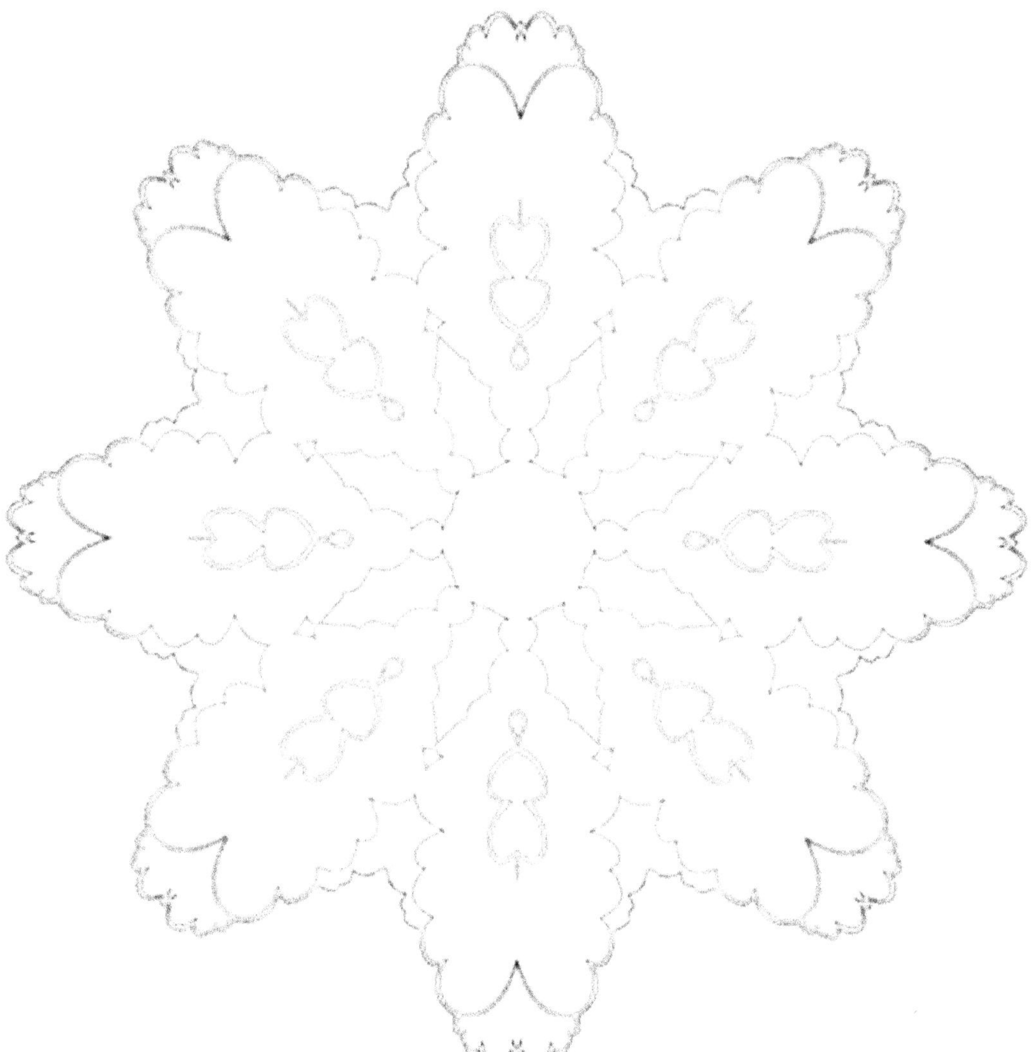

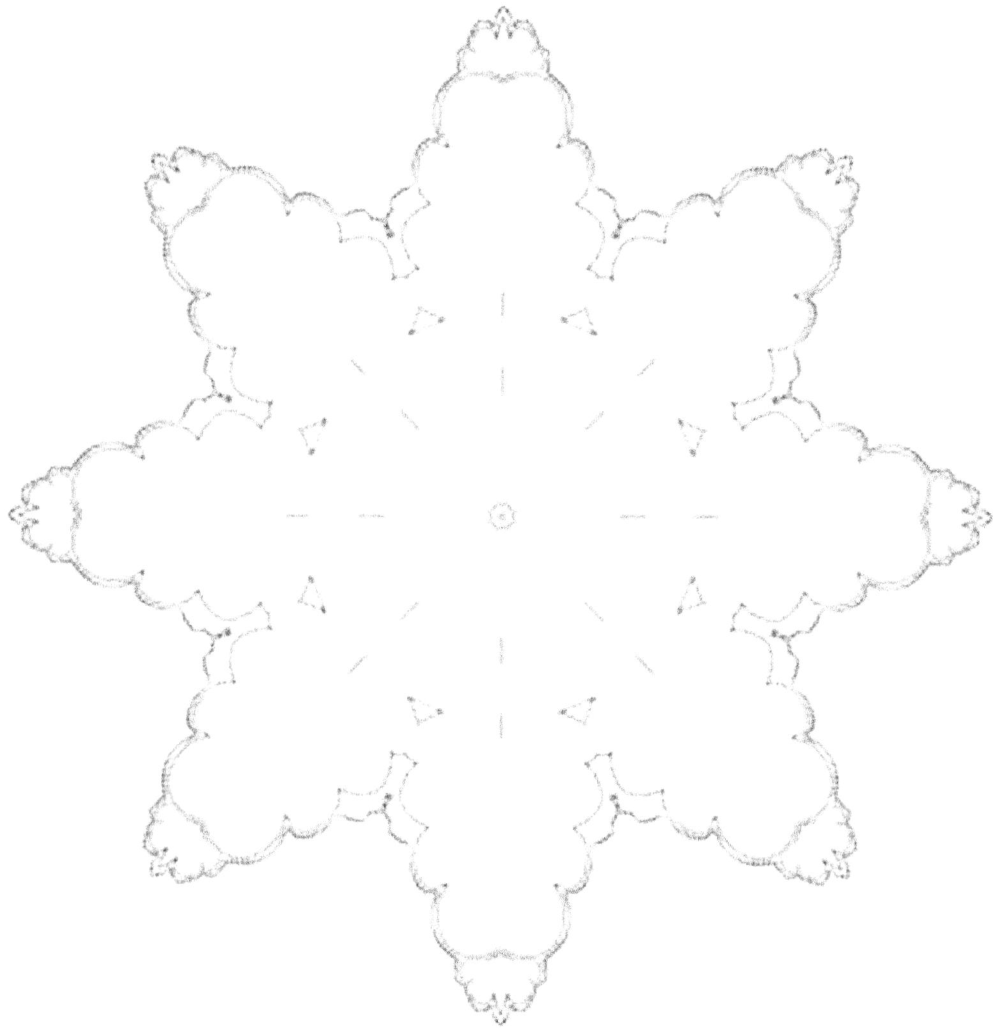

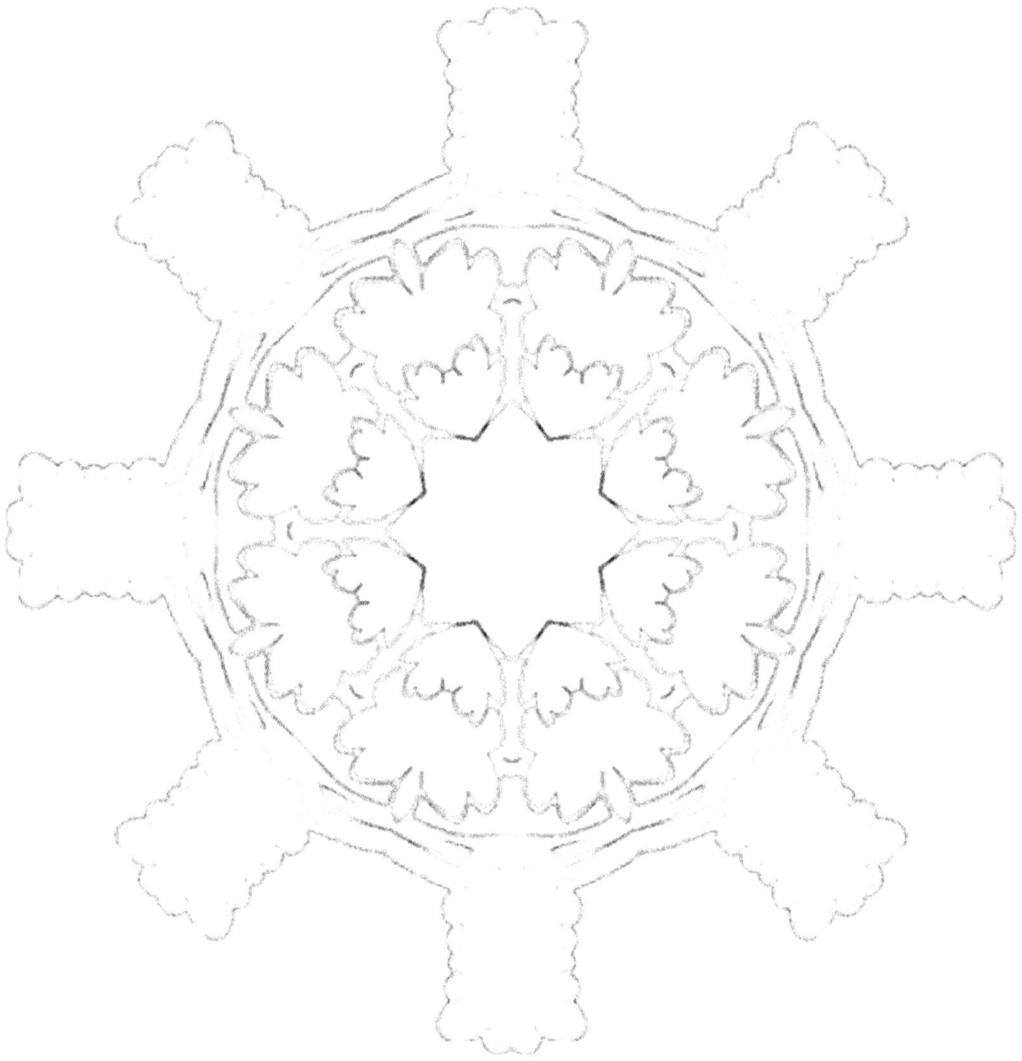

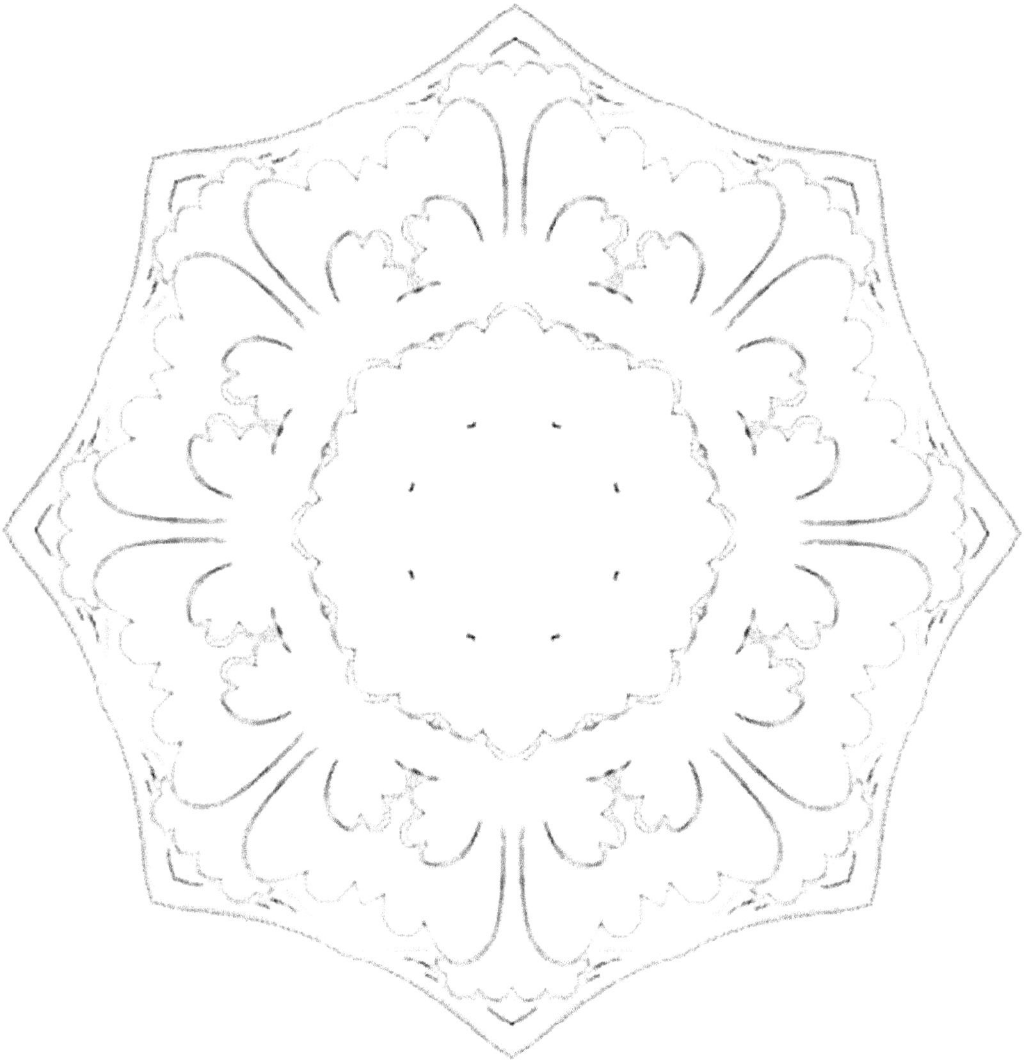

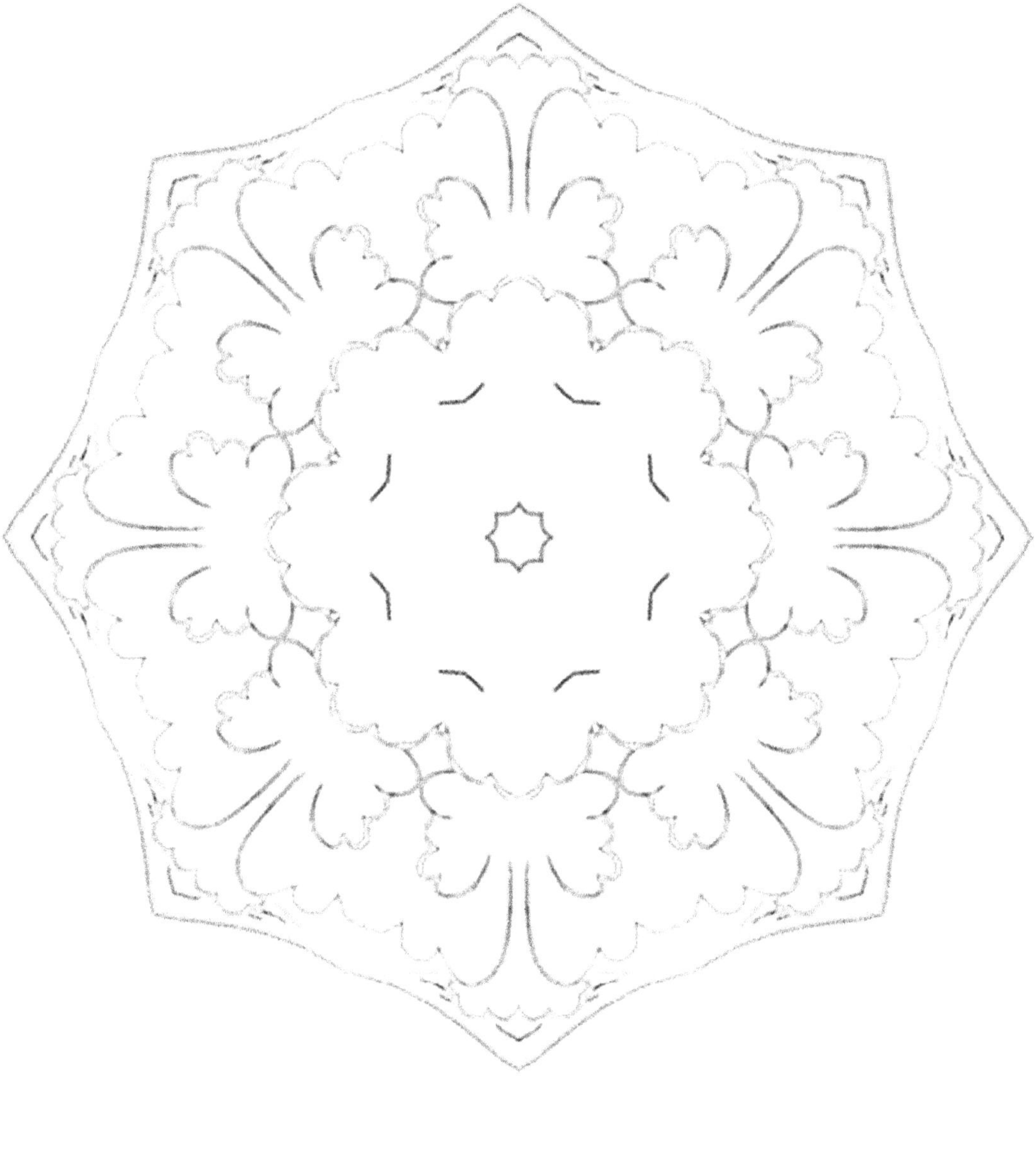

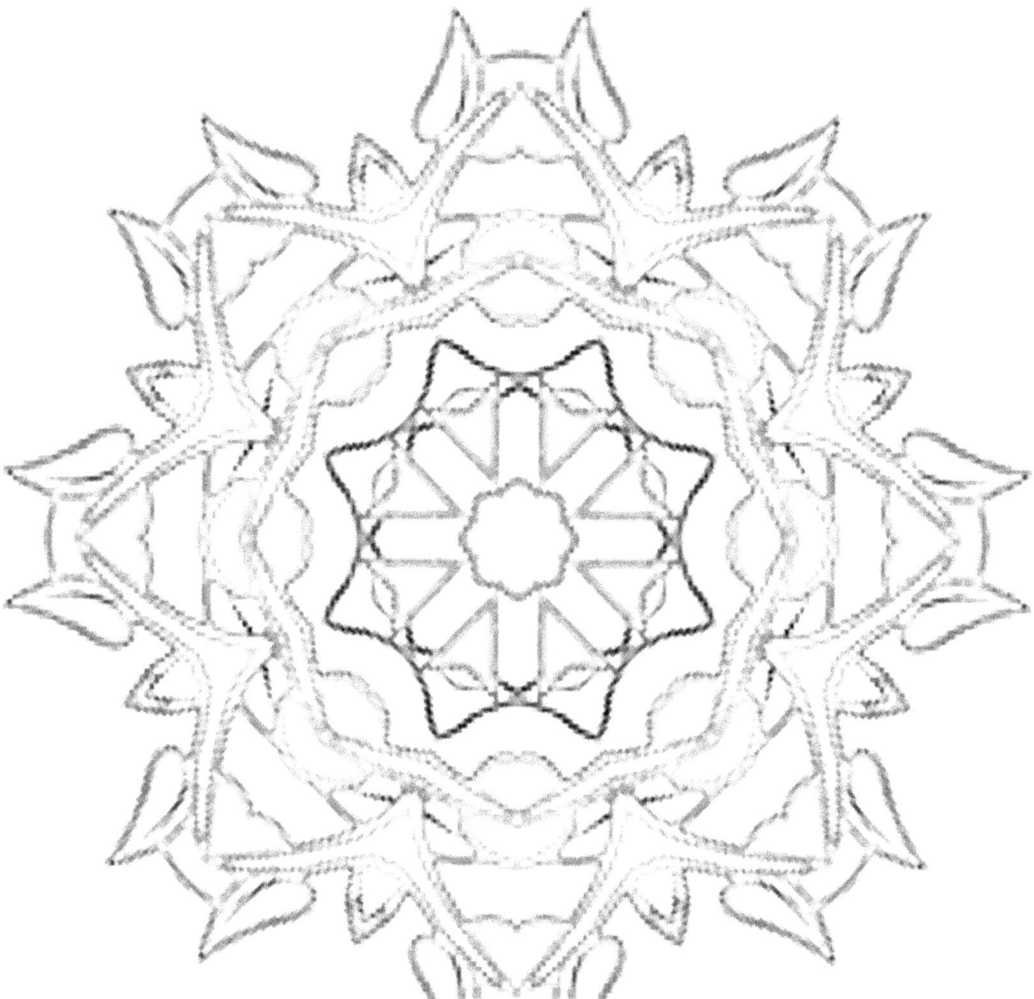

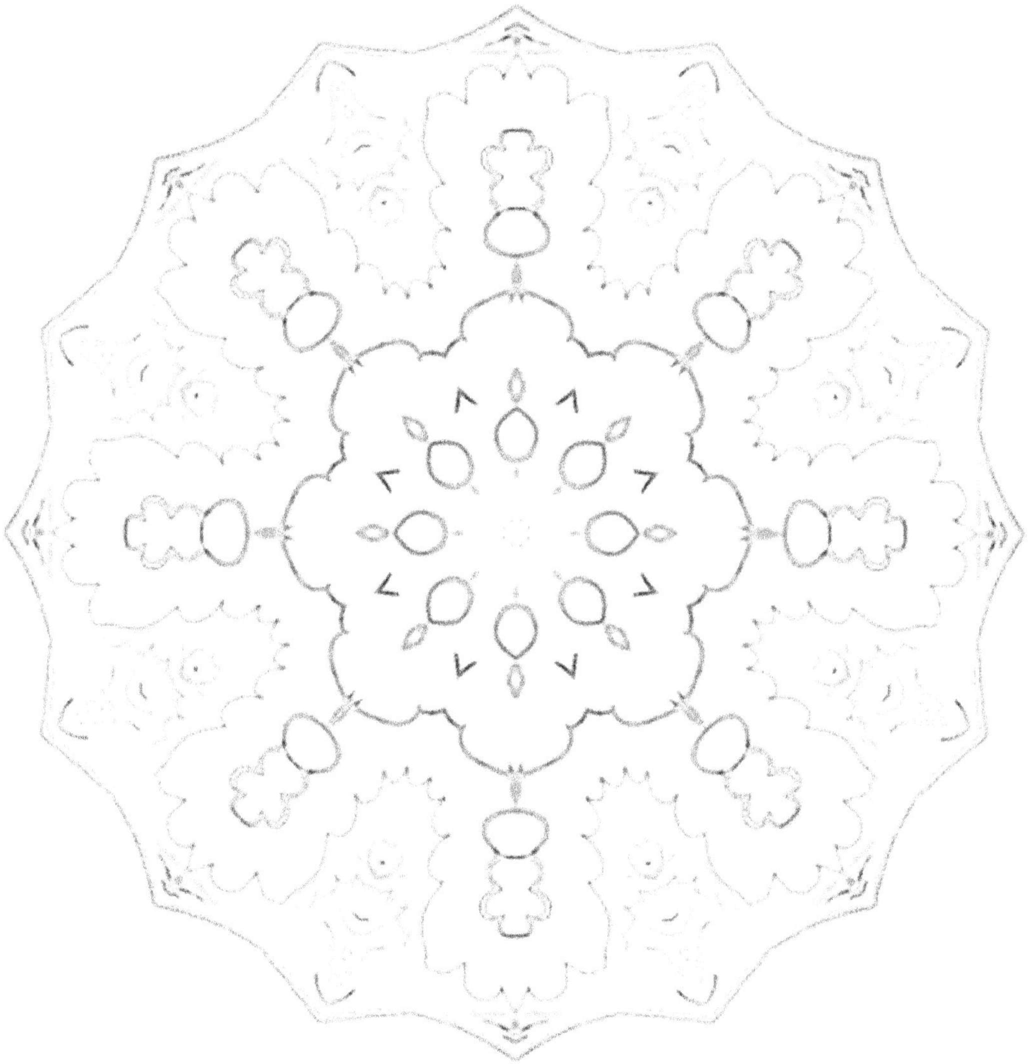

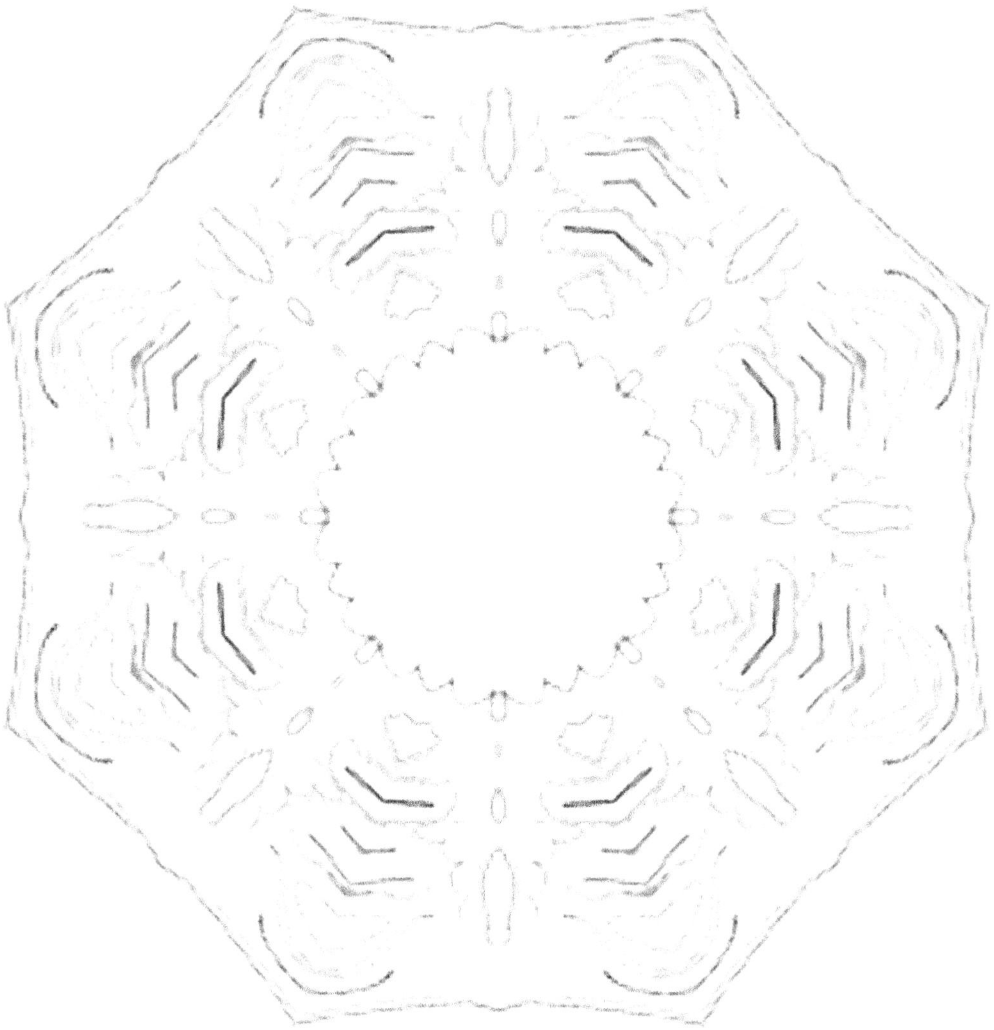

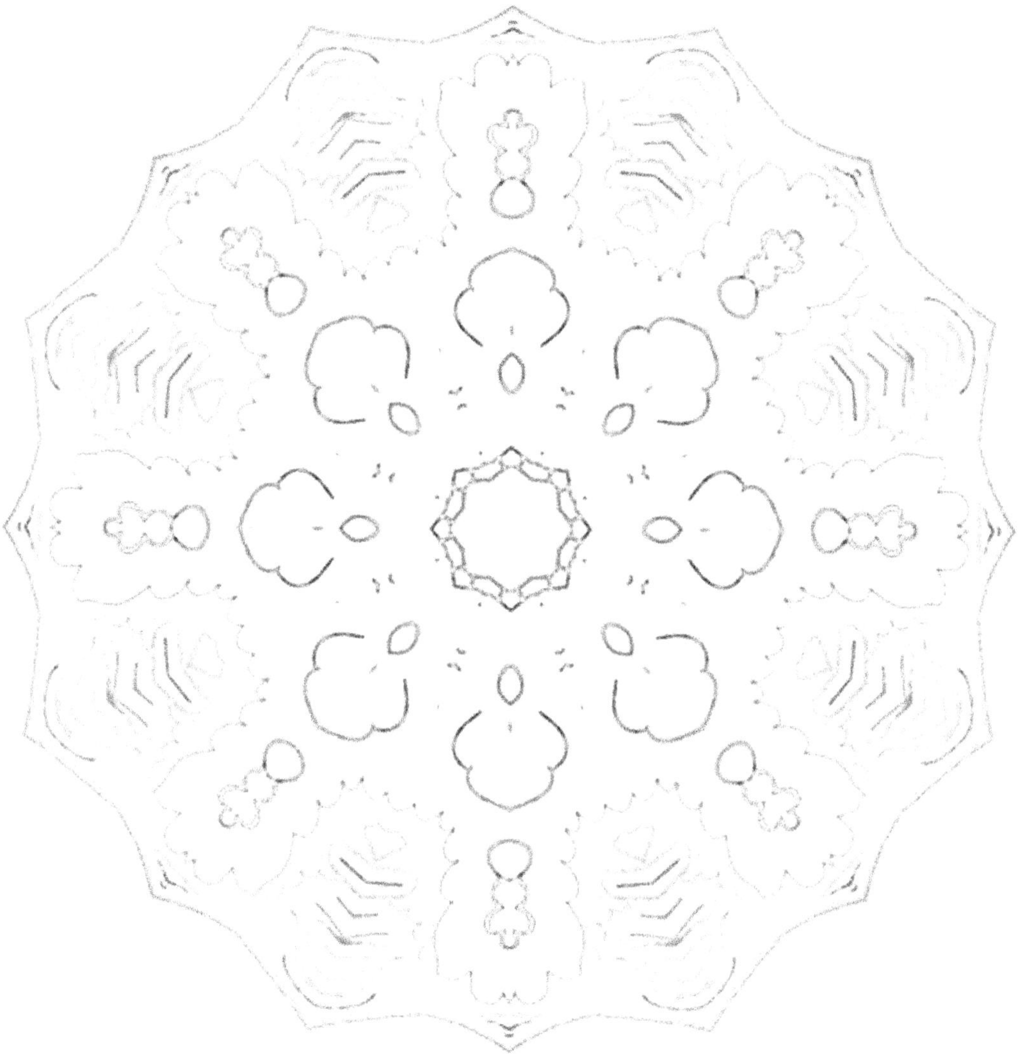

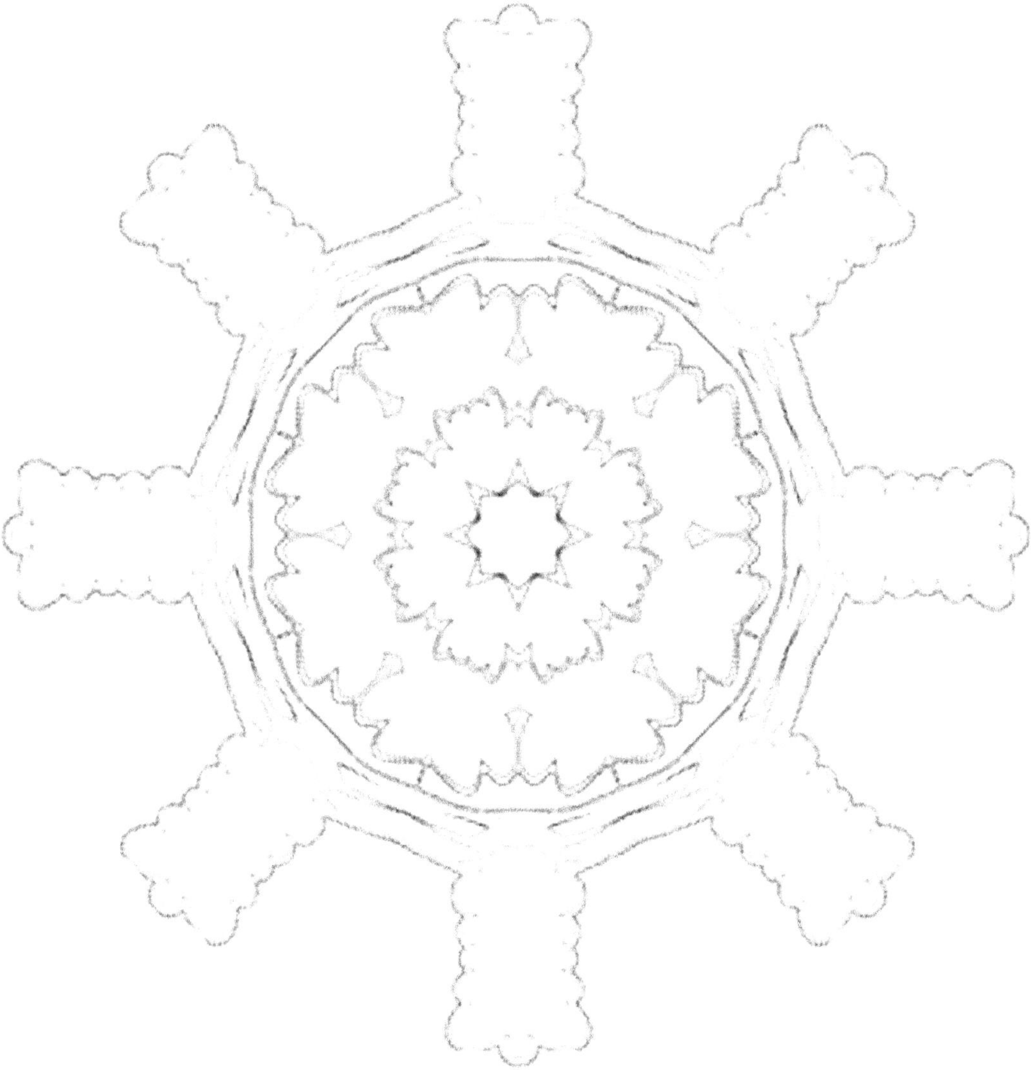

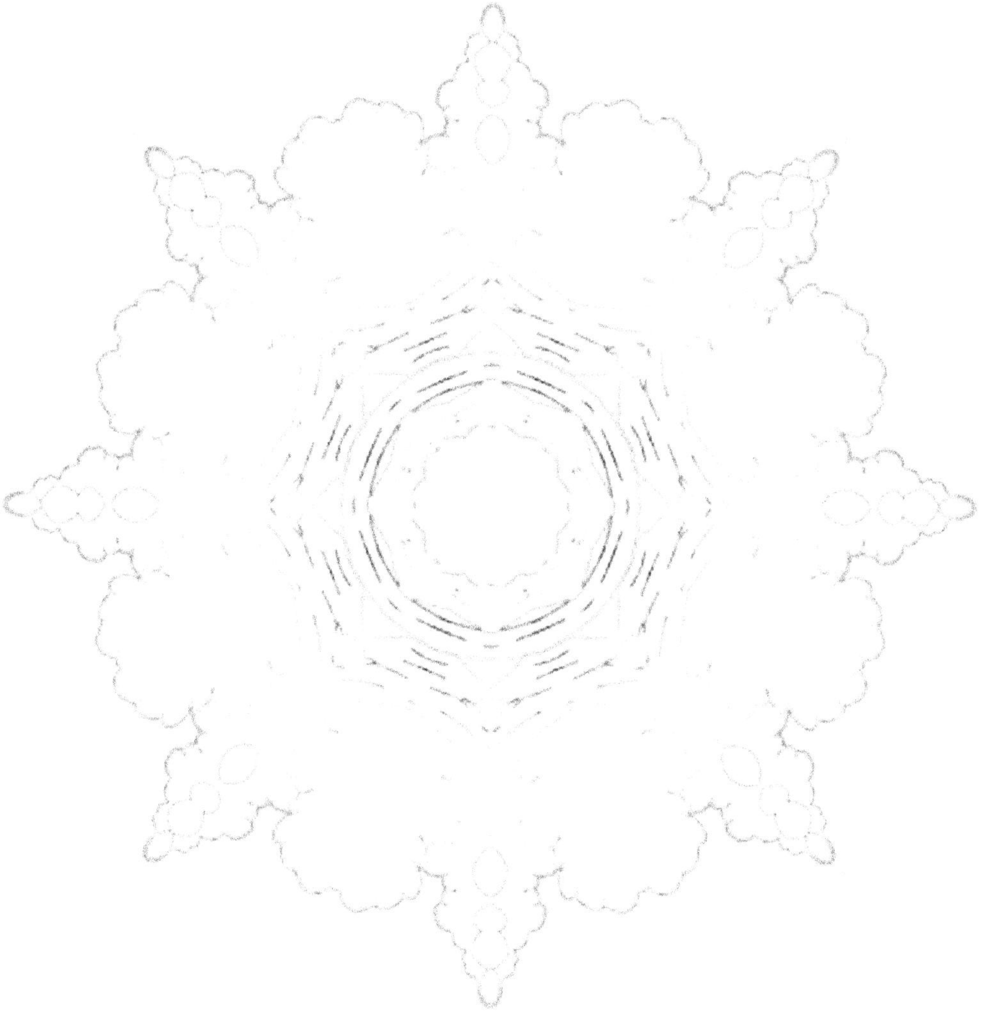

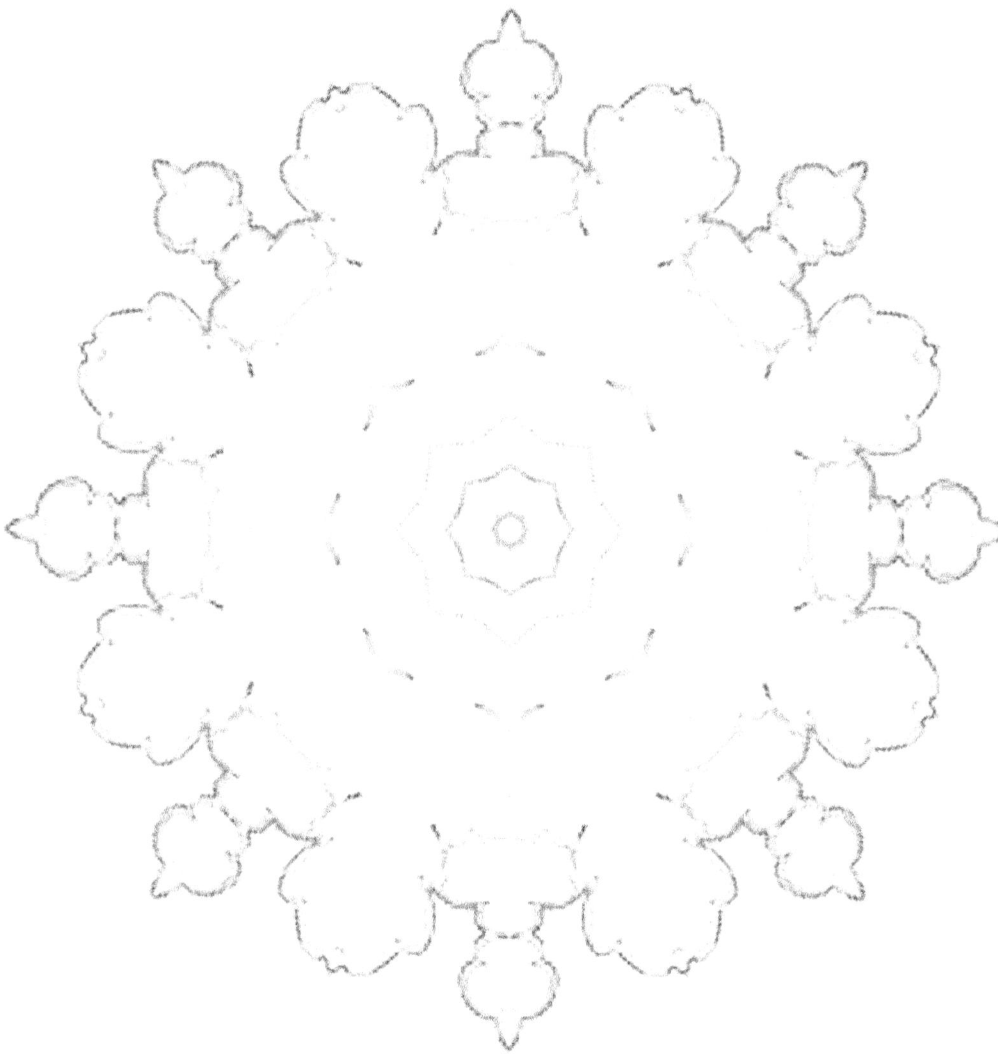

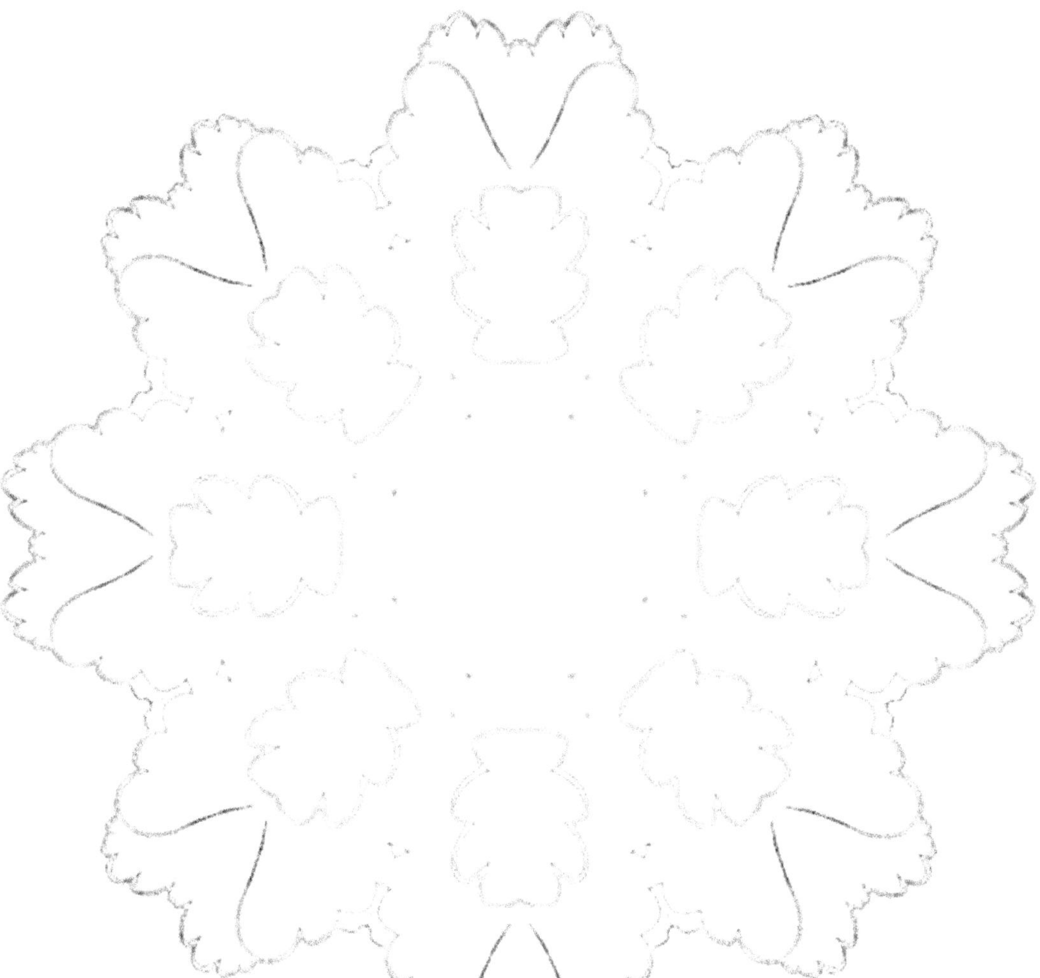

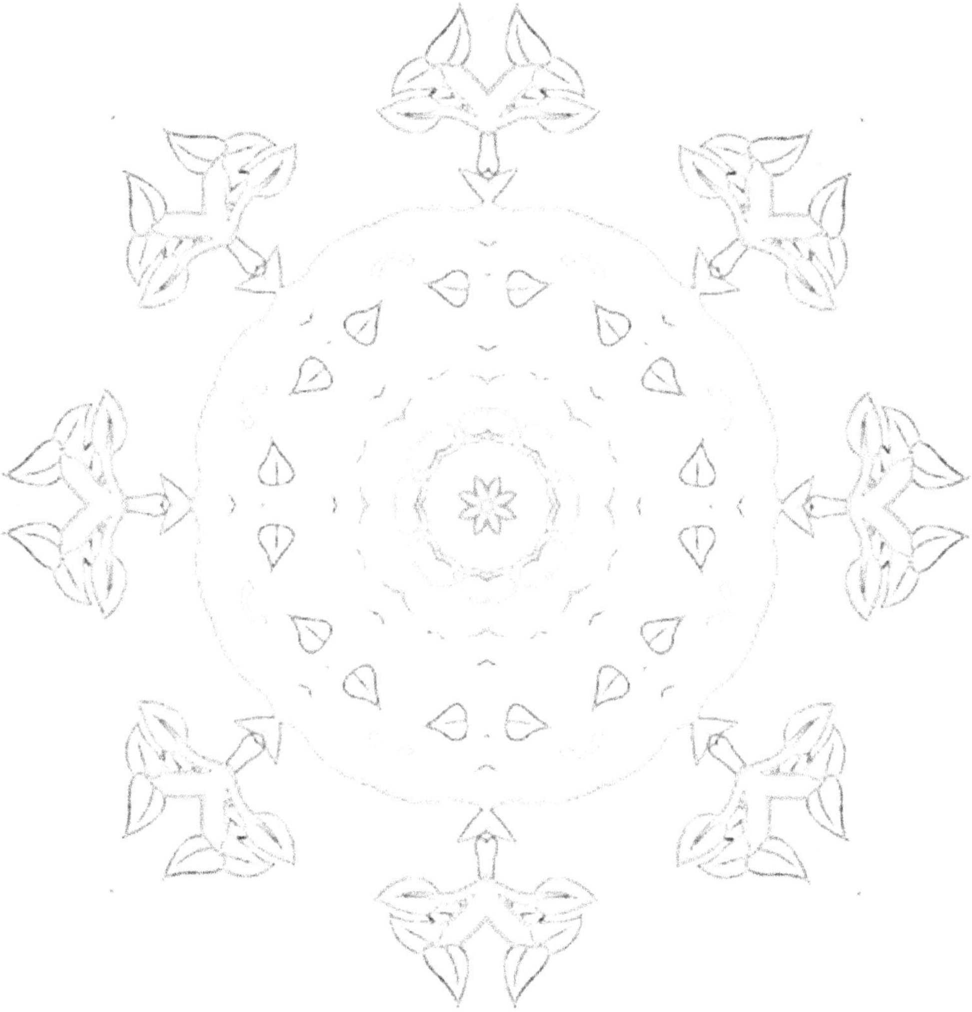

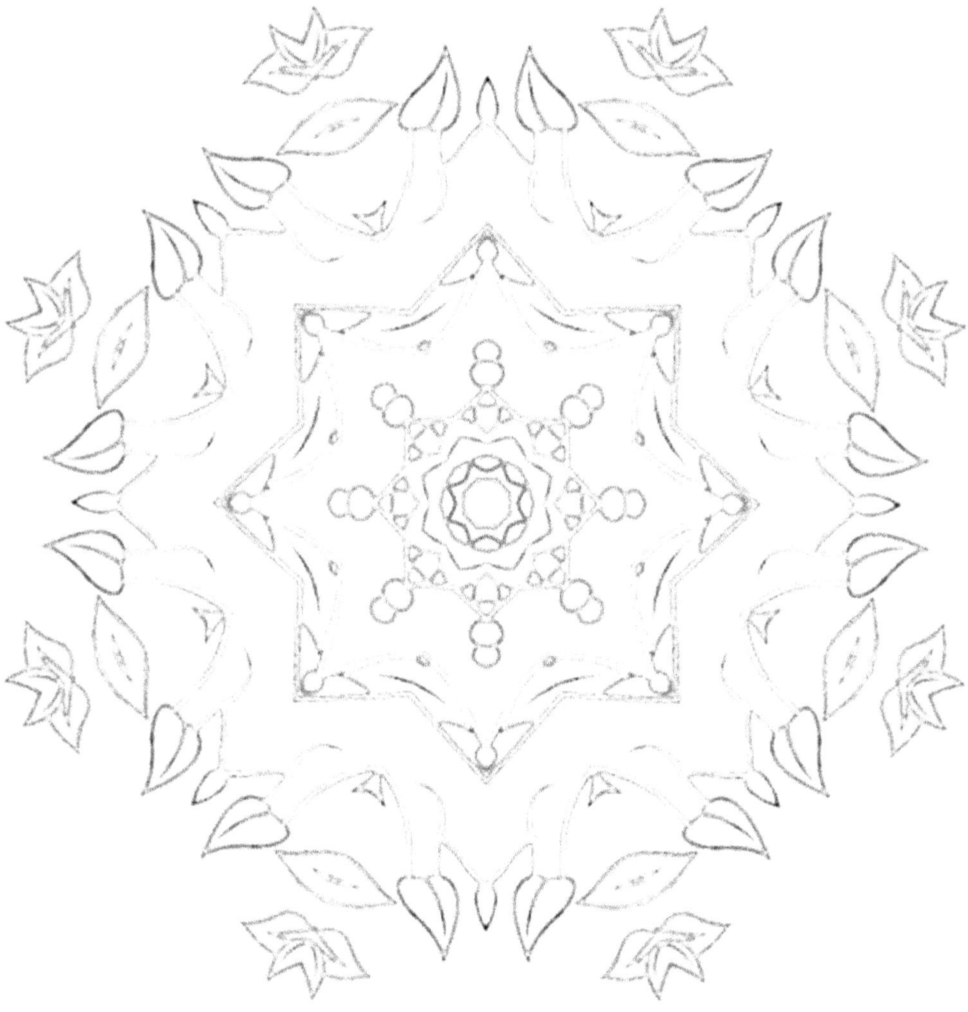

Note

www.ingramcontent.com/pod-product-compliance
Lightning Source LLC
Chambersburg PA
CBHW080650180526
45168CB00008B/3374